warm blooded things

warm blooded things

Shaun Hill

Nine
Arches
Press

warm blooded things
Shaun Hill

ISBN: 978-1-913437-21-3
eISBN: 978-1-913437-22-0

First published December 2021 by:

Nine Arches Press
Unit 14, Sir Frank Whittle Business Centre,
Great Central Way, Rugby.
CV21 3XH
United Kingdom

www.ninearchespress.com

Printed in the United Kingdom by:
Imprint Digital

Nine Arches Press is supported using public funding by Arts Council England.

Supported using public funding by
**ARTS COUNCIL
ENGLAND**

Contents

III.

your whole life is a series of embedded urgencies.
– Mark Fisher

what if I film my way out?
– Guy Madden

maps of light

we sacrifice so much to survive.
use fingers as weak shields for the face.
we can't grow limbs back like a salamander can.
but we can go back and gather. whisper: *I am so lucky.*

we are the descendants of plants. a million
different paths mapping the mathematics of light.
cut this stem you've stepped into. see how it isn't stone.

now turn it. find an edge. don't dig yourself a death yet.
there is someone inside you who never left.
gripping the carpet of your lungs.
waiting alone in the dark.

I.

castaway

all those nights alone. barely
dipping your feet in the living
room you were tethered to.

bulb in remote
blinking morse code –
but you couldn't see it.

you forced your mind
through glass in hope
you'd float to the other side.

group-sleep aboard the
night-ship to Coventry

in a glass dome at the edge of the world,
that's where you'll find him:
splitting mist as he steers this
steel forge toward sleep.

past the green blur of a service station
with tin barbeques in stacks;
gold arches, the promise
of high-fat happiness.

past the swiped screen of towerblocks,
their pixelated faces;
into a red-eyed sky-line
of offices, cranes –

wishing at his window seat
he could dissolve and discover love.
but then who would ride the night-ship?
kick-drum the rhythm of the night shift?

hear the black ticking hand strain
to wipe away the rain?

burnt bulbs

rows of seats like black teeth in a dead shark's mouth.
I flick popcorn into a blue bag with a small metal broom.

the screen is a white sheet a film wears like a ghost.
I've been scraping gum off the steps of this Adele album

for weeks. white noise fizzing on a dead shark's tongue.
black T and blue badge with someone else's name.

but I set fire to the rain... at 2 am, I'll stagger into light
to tell you why: *I'm sorry. I love you. I hate me.*

sanctuary

I'm looking for a way in
to your life; knocking
on a mirror to find
a hidden room behind it.

can you buzz me in?
can you text me the code?
am I on the list? no?
can you say you know me?

it's me. you know me.
I wrote you a message
in mist on the glass, tap
back if you can read it.

help me make a bridge of a bruise.

workshopping

some people go for months   without touch
sat in cafés   sometimes I get so lonely I beg
the internet for sex   one night I straddled
an unmade mattress on the floor   on grindr
but not for dick   had friends but not for pity
I needed to be touched in the gap that only art
can bridge   white vice tightening with each
long minute   I arranged to meet a stranger
a philosophy PhD   to sit beside him writing
at a pub   forty minutes later: *meet me at
mine?* he typed   *I'll give you a blowjob*   I
told a straight friend the story and he laughed:
what did you   expect?   the irony of being
employed   (however tenuously)   to create
space for connection   and failing to facilitate
any without some form   of excuse: clipboard
to point to as I knock on doors   in a universe
of rented rooms   cupboards full of food.

witnesses

she stood with a booklet cupped in her gloved
hands like the last limp leaf on a tree, arm to arm
on the pavement, with the others, in silence –
a mini library beside them – cold yet content
with being there, visible. who's the real vulgar
preacher here? bent over a page like a plate
at a buffet, begging you to believe me: *I know
the way to save you...* I don't want to save you.

I don't.   I do but I won't.

hunger

the street is whistling to the animal in me,
calling my name in all directions. I'm tired
of being manipulated, tired of pacing circles
in concrete looking for lunch I can't afford;
rolling dice with the road until I can't tread
another step, and the grey sky shatters like
a rubik's cube – and nothing left to do but
kneel in a puddle of who I have to be now.

a man steps from a corso and closer to ask
if I'm okay, if l was praying. I feel the same
shiver of need in him: wind in a back alley,
burden he carries as he shoulders a bucket
of soil from a skip, a wish – to shift gears,
to limp here unsteered and be – breathing
beneath the wet yellow leaves of a tree, sap
below the skin of knuckles pushed to bark.

like the lifeguard who told me he told his wife
he was taking the dog for a walk and forgot
to bring the dog with him. his hard body bent
on a car by a reservoir, deep voice wobbling:
I need this… city revving softly in his throat.
and this man, keys in hand, reaching tenderly
again to ask: *are you okay?* I have my own guilt.
no space for yours. I nod once and walk away.

hydrodynamics
for Lizz

trying to hold it
in, all week –
what about release?

did you not hear? water
can power small cities for a day.

so pull back the curtain
and climb inside the rain.

green thumb
you are bleeding and
you need to wash your hands.

dressing room

in the absence of a camera a mirror
is turned against another, so the body
split between them will begin to police itself.

the woman at the till flashing red on her wrist
reveals something in the psyche. the man
in the street selling balloons lets go.

this is your uniform: sipping water on knees
so no customer can see; eyes rebooting
for each, as if you're Marina at MoMA.

this is what a uniform is: a thing to mark
a boundary – the counter between us
we take with us, in us, on but never off.

puppet

my sock puppet is sad. it talks
about depression for money.
cries about capitalism. shows
drunk strangers its buttonholes.

my sock puppet has a pipe
cleaner bent into a moustache.
my sock puppet is a portrait
Lorca made of Salvador Dali.

my puppet collects compliments
but has no pockets to keep them.
my puppet is a big fat piggy
bank spilling out self-worth.

my tinder date begs me to keep
my sock on during sex. puppet
·says *yes!* I stare at the ceiling.
the bed creaks beneath my fist.

my puppet has shame stitched
into its skin. my puppet never
quite fits. now I can't remember
what my real fingers feel like.

I need to be real for a minute.
strip me from within of this
urge to be perfect. I haven't
rested my thumb in months.

my puppet wears me like string
flapping on a threadbare scarf.

opulent monk

a bidding war for my body between two men on the phone:
he offered more but I want you... I say, then fuck them both.
life gets dirty when you've got books to buy and debt to pay
but your sugar daddy's stingy. Tuesdays I clean a bungalow
where I listen to a podcast (*On Being with Krista Tippett*)
wearing a puppy butt plug and getting beat by a cane.
so I broke another precept, call me an opulent monk.
trust me, it's a righter kind of livelihood to pickling drunk
wankers at a gala bar – thirty-foot-black-curtains draped
in a cushy cave at the NEC: champagne tray on my wrist,
bruised shoes that do not fit, nodding for hours to be tipped
a crumb of a minute's wage. so he injects crack into his leg
he's given me the money, it's chill. I lean up the wall
as he flips the bed and for just a second think he'll kill me.
he held his fist to my chin for so long it became a goatee –
now who's your daddy? I try to meditate on the bus ride home.

nightwalking in Exeter

some nights I'd walk myself alive.
let the street decide. I came this close.

(dull halo of a megabus down a dual carriageway)

tried to let go of the railings. lips
grazing a lorry. *you should*. I couldn't.

(cold wind clicking on a crane's metal cage)

thought I'd slip into the river. rip this
letter I up. but my tongue became a torch.

(blue discus of an ambulance hurtling through the dark)

push your ear to the breath of it.
resuscitate a reason.

II.

life round here

where the grass is green and the / kids
smoke hash and the teens get / smashed.

where the rent is high and the / people
poor and their washing machines / break.

where the cure for a headache is a / hard
on and the men inside serve / time.

where the gas goes fast and guilt / slow
we live next door to / death.

has it become any easier to love each other?

unzip the door in torchlight
and crawl down next to me.
make a home here in the mud,
temporarily. two voices resting
together like rope. this is what
we remembered and spoke
into words for the first time:

faggot. snapping
like elastic. a boy's fists.
I need to know I exist.
a pocket of change.
my father's rage. honestly,
I had to. *I wasn't proud
to love you.* but I loved you.

boys like you

your father skinned your head so you wouldn't remind him
of your mother. hair clings to carpet as if it were feathers
of a broken thing: chin down after finding out it couldn't fly.

jaw mouthing a pride that matches the red and white flag
of baggy tracksuits they wear. tough meat is preferred here.
and this is why boys like you disappear. but you know this.

teeth meet knuckles in this place. cheek on a chain fence.
glass pebbles in the dirt. you think a smile is just a shape
the moon makes. how quickly you forget how to fidget.

how to stage a hate crime

when he spat in my face and the others
got off the bus to beat me, I got back on.
close the door. please just close the door.

they stood there on the pavement,
laughing at me: poofter on a screen.
I'm sorry. excuse me, can I sit here?

she pulled her coat close. they all did.
turned their heads as if my face
were contagious. *they... I...*

I closed my eyes. held myself
the whole way, like the last time.

song of the first men

I board a bus to the city beneath
the tunnels under train-lines

pass the chapel of chapped brick
and drop down in the crypt

dig the dirt and deeper through
lose my nails until I find

solid proof that the myths were true
that the men were once alive.

wet-plate process

I.

on the back of a Kingston bus we brush hands below a waistband
and like the rush of blood we rise on a spinning disc in the dark

and in that crease of buckled skin prying eyes cannot distinguish
the leap of dreams bucking high on a spinning disk in the dark

and in the street the suspension of a leaf above a puddle,
moon in a milk bottle as we ride on a spinning disc in the dark

but when we release our fingers tip-toe time into a fugue
and pass the man who tried to capture an image of life

on a spinning disc in the dark, as a spinning disc in the dark.

II.

if love only exists if someone's saying it's there
then maybe that's the point of photography,
how in the room behind an eyelid light can

find a way to develop in the dark: first as
red to a wound, then bruised iris beside it,
the yellow thirst of sleep's tongue lapping

at a tear-duct, before the heavy fall to all
four feet up in the air, until it's impossible
to tell or tear the earth from the sky.

III.

aren't you the man who told me
horses could glide?

their hooves the thumping force
inside a human heart?

I need to believe

your words are more than just
clapped coconut

on a spinning disc in the dark
on a spinning disc in the dark.

underground

beneath the cave-painting of a cubicle-wall,
with its smudge of numbers and nazi-signs,

he lies his head on the tile and pushes
an ear into the cold

fossil of another man's handprint,
and imagines him
                              wild and unashamed.

before a disease blistered
all that history between them:

fingers squeezing snow
into something they can hold,

both their tongues tied
under a train…

        under and over and over again.

wood and water

to lie blind like this in a maze where
each turn is a freezing wall of dirt:
cocooned in regret, cocooned in a life
where death is the only transformation.

each rib rippling to slip the next one
on to split frost with a muscular nose,
but it can't – the harsh world turns –
a man in a street who sleeps in his coat.

a robin burrowing into her red chest
on a twig-twine nest in a low wind.
a fire's yellow dome and a dog's loose
orbit in the cold blue world beyond it.

are we not responsible for each other?

look

I.

cheap wine spilt on the steps of a church.
a small tent of hands shield a fresh-lit wick.
and sputtering truth the young
priest releases incense.
on the bottom step I confess
I want to paint a mural
on the roof of my mouth too.
I want to crouch down into a choir
of *yes* and open myself to the holy.
put the moon out with a cigarette,
make it day again. grind polystyrene
into snow and feed my pity to the pigeons.
break free from the fingers I am peeking
through. this urge to look and to not.

II.

he pointed at the red brick steeple through his windshield:
tower where the priest had thrown himself when he found
out he had AIDS. my eyes dropped the distance to pavement,
feeling the one long second it took for him to fall there.

I was sat in traffic with a vicar I'd met a few months before
on an app, who kept his flat unlatched for me, after my shifts
at the last dive open in the city – stairs into earth, gay underworld
with a pole on a stage in the middle; glitter on the curb

from when a girl slashed another girl's leg with a glass.
that night, with my butch friend Becky in the back and me
stacking lemons on shots of tequila, I'd lean closer to hear
the stuttered words of a body sobbing into a double brandy.

III.

I wanted a compass to god but only
got pointed back to my country,
downing gin in a doilied living room
with the monarchy on the mantelpiece.
I wanted a window: wisdom. got a mouth
reflecting my own addictions. I needed
those big hands around me, my name
on his knuckles. instead, I knelt naked
in bed with a man too fucked on wine
to fuck me. I knelt at a candle bench
with a broken lighter and no matches
to turn to: the panes of men's faces
sliding free of their screws until all
that's left was the frame of a house
I was running from in the first place.

fast trance trickling into beige

hunched in a dim-lit kitchen sniffing
bliss off the back of a hand. black
eye. his two big pupils. faces blurring
into one blue winter. he swallowed
snow with his father and had never
felt closer. he was faraway.
hunched in a dim-lit kitchen sniffing
bliss off the back of a hand. black
eye. *his* two big pupils. faces blurring
once again together. he swallowed
snow with his son and had never
felt closer. he was faraway. running
fifty laps around a car park in the dark.
pushing the small red button saying: *wait.*

that night, I saw god under a traffic light

he told me how he'd had to leave his wife and son that week.
dreams that drop him in a ditch of cold sweat in the night.
how they're better off without him: without him, a better life.
I offered him a rollie. he said they made him think of burnt hair

and we are there: shrapnel and mist, dead friends fizzing
around him like leaves; a body twisting against his camo vest
but he can't get close enough, he's using his bare hands
to put out the little girl on fire – and I remember him

reaching with raw eyes underneath a traffic light: guilt
for the part he played, hunger and hatred for himself; grief
is a heavy thing that's difficult to put down, even now
he's handing me this story, as if to say: *hold her.*

hold me warm blooded thing

in this midst of this *I love you sometimes*
we were pleading the way the dying do:

hold me warm blooded thing.
hold me like the other men
who are not silent round a coffin.

lips blue as frozen strawberries soon
we are bleeding the way the living do:

hold me warm blooded thing.
hold me as if touch exists
as if it isn't just another myth.

I put your fingers in my mouth the way
I think I'm supposed to, so why don't you

hold me warm blooded thing?
hold me how a body does a name,
how a pin holds down a grenade.

yes, we're a magnet for disaster the way
the earth is at its poles, but I need you to

hold me warm blooded thing
until I'm nothing but weeping,
until I'm nothing but water and salt.

bridge (Great Charles Street Queensway)

from here, in this longed-for geometry,
I can finally see you how the pigeons do,
perching on cold air until it whispers:

we are one. I'm watching the cars tie
a knot in the night. I needed to see it.
how inside each hood is a bump of air,

each ribbon-red flare a life. Birmingham,
I can feel your blood hum beneath my feet.
carry this poem to where the dead can hear me.

why do I think your death belongs to me?

you – who went to the hospital and came back
with a haircut. who gathered the harvest to have it
rot in your arms. with wok in hand, who batted smoke
pellets back through a window. with a hoop on
each finger: brown cherubs glittered with salt.
limping toward a finish line in dry-eyed delirium.
derailed train scattering cows toward a lake.
little bee, bombarded by rain. ballistic missile.
missing person. shredded kite. my kind.
each morning. muscle. bruise. burn. termites
ticking a log to nothing. fists dripping links of gold
chain in a divot in the dirt. one day wrists will
wheel their last stack of words across a page.
– me? I'm the woman with the green gloves
clipping ivy from the graves.

time spun loosely into a beautiful day

i.m. Leon Priestnall

the dead shock
-wave away from us,
ripples in a necklace of water.

we want so much to be so much
and so much for each other.

white ball tossed
through the cold air
to crinkle off the rim of a bin.

death cracks the nut of a body
and the wisps lift up to love.

Leon, who laid a blue rug
for us to sit on and weep –

to spin the volume
like a dial on a safe, fling
open our mouths to sing:

*let the sunshine, let the sun
shine in, the sun is shining…*

to release rage like spit
valves on a trumpet and
tired-eye-trudge toward it.

the house is deflating

lit-wick in an abandoned mine –
he stutters into a spliff, waiting
for the hiss of his oven
to come in and claim him.

tears drip on bare feet
as he sits there in the black,
waiting to hear the lock turn,
but dad, we're gone.

III.

sleeping on stilts in the Irish Sea

leg dangled like a cigarette
off the metal edge of a rig.

beam from a helmet falling
into the open mouth of a wave.

sea tossing up its lips to kiss
the bottom of a boot.

tensing up its tongue to touch
the dream of being deliberate.

tapping at piano keys to stay alive

we stared from the edge of our own dark heads
but I could never really touch your sadness:
feet bruised playing blue piano – or was that me?
I too have clung to the earth with a single screw
left in a lifting hinge. I leant a chair over
a pit for years: controlled demolition pushed
back another week. did *you* relearn how to walk?
to slowly make each step feel real as the years
of near survival? the grasp of gravity more
than a cheap knock-off of the real thing?
feet leave a trace when you step from
a shower, have blisters, can be dusted
at the crime-scene of a life just as easy
as prints, to show scratches, lonely,
4 am walking habits, the bad posture…

is that the real thing?

forward

drifting like a drunk on a dancefloor
only I no longer drink; sleep presses pause
on this quick living: this honey-thick slip
stream of one life to the next we're leaping
like salmon against, scraping rock raw on
the long fall down. rockpool, jug on a boulder
wall I grip with both hands: blood beckoning
adrenaline, a vague sense of blue vicissitude,
like hanging in a lift shaft watching death
slide and all you can do is climb, lean into
a direction and trust time to take you there.

metal lid that hides the sky

I check the time – two *Lord of the Rings* of the shift left –
and stare up at the six-foot sign hung on a far wall:
green man stepping through a door of white light,
exiting a fire and entering something, exiting a fire
and entering something, exiting a fire and entering

the unhinged mouth of a snake swallowing itself,
thoughts of escape repeated until time ceases
to have meaning. two people inside me now
(it's exhausting) riding the thin ridge between
worker and witness, suspended in quantum

superposition, mind glancing back into fire
whilst my body is cracking to ash inside it.
it would be easier this way: surrender to each
new face and serve my purpose. *yes sir, no sir.*
single-use smiles squeezed out of a tube. *I do.*

no. I refuse to be exploited twice. I'll hack what
these bastards gave me: architecture, archetype,
green man hung from the rigging and become him.
alien. no-name-big-brain beamed into black tie
to observe how life moves on this strange planet.

fresco

after Federico García Lorca

grey,
this city of grey,
this city of rain-
soaked cardboard.
this city of gargoyles
in shop doorways
with their skinny hands reaching.

grey,
mosaic of grey
slab after slab
of the way we live.
the slap of feet
on pavement,
the slip of cards into machines.

and green,
that dream of green,
the dreaming trees
in this city of glass.
if I stepped into that
mirror would I find me
finding my own slow way to grace?

grace,
the armless grace
of a mannequin
plinthed in streetlight,
staring you in the eye
and simply
smiling, asking for nothing.

the raw edge we left when
we tore our eyes away

what happened is I saw her: smiling in her seat –
head back in a hammock hung from here to happy.
what happened is she saw me: wheeling a bike
along the platform in the rain, staring into joy,
and she was ashamed. this country can bully us
until we don't let each other see we're shining,
until we don't let life in for weeks but now
look at us dance: spinning kayak of she-looks,
then-I-look, until we both look ridiculous,
until I'm a woman beaming at her fogged-up
reflection, until we're twin-fish rubbing lungs
with the world, no hazmat suit to keep us
from touching within; glass collapsing to mist
as the train released its breaks to drift away,
and I want to thank you stranger, for that stray
bullet of beauty, sting called courage, an answer.

to be educated

for bell hooks

I walked through the windy street quick
then slow, as the page began to dim
in the space between each lamppost –
so much love burns up before we touch it,
life flailing for slim meaning, but in a book
we can bubble up to this place: new
mind, next page, this is all it takes.

I wrote a list, poured days into blocks,
small cubes popped from a tray to drop
in my year and sip through the weeks,
to dip in and up from the ripple of us,
lean in and listen to the mighty love
of a stranger who spent years alone
so I would know I never will be.

and so with truth brimming in my ears
I flicked through dishes in the sink, learning
to braid her pain with my pain like a wire
to a fuse, to spark a light that might sustain
the pause between the things I think
and say: the space for you, to know yourself
as more than just that pain, to be educated.

if this is all a story, why can't it be a good one?

I tucked a receipt against a page, tossing down whatever pamphlet
I was making a ladder of that morning, reaching for my own voice,
and saw her: stashed like a corpse beneath the bracketed shelf.

she'd stashed herself. eyes closed for *just a moment*. her thin coat
stained; feet splayed śavāsana. I feared for her. what else could I do
but mutter *no no no* in my head and wait for the worst? I worked

my eyes back through the stacks to an empty white desk mapping
the steps of a librarian who would circle back here and evict her.
there he was: side on, arm swinging back and forth. I watched him

pendulum the frame at the top of the stairs running errands
in the children's section. and another one: pink-haired woman
with her back to us clearing a trolley of trashy-thrillers. I looked

around at my society, everyone of them an enemy, and waited
to release my hatred – but no bomb went off. no threats to call
the police. no teary pleas to stay. they simply passed her body by.

loaned her sore limbs some warmth for the hours. held space.
how quick my own body tried to block our becoming, staging
some pre-written scene where a glitch into harm is always

inevitable; clinging to the word *radical* like a torn red towel –
I swore we're all matadors to one form of violence or another,
anticipating an ending, clapping when we mean to intervene.

three members of staff closing in, their backs blocking sky…
metal doors clapping shut like the serrated jaws of a cage…
all tills suddenly still as a man in a shop began to shout.

how he spun around at the crowd of baskets pinning him in
to perspective, eyes signalling concern via easy solemnity,
heads shook softly at the desperate man with his fist raised:

what a shame. sealing him into the pit of his already limited
decisions, we knew were shaped by forces, forces we could
interrupt – red threads in the air that led me there: lunch

plans with a man who bought me books I couldn't afford,
a detour (road closure on Broad Street,) lurching off the hot
bus early, to stand in that store holding a cold bottle of water,

before entering the heat of it, the white heat of the moment,
thin edge where events intersect and step forward into real time,
inside the exact second where the man at last prepares to punch

and be between them, palm up to the three, my other forming
an ark to surround and receive him, to hold him as I would
another me, my whole quiet being beaming: *this is my human.*

I held him and felt the heat in us quickly return to human,
and they received me; me: this skinny-gay-man-boy offering
a real choice – pocket of air in the timeline of poverty and shame,

to breathe and ask if he really wanted, or needed, to do it –
and he chose this, heading for the doors with my body beside his,
where he left the three in peace and me stepping out stunned

to walk: still dizzy from sun stroke, forgetting my bottle of water,
jacked up on adrenaline until the elastic band of what happened
snapped and I began to weep – this was *goodness* and it filled me!

like that morning in the library when a girl tugged on sleeves to ask:
dad, why are they doing that? and he breathed. *because she's a person.*
she needs to lie down. and I knew then, how even a bankrupt shack

on the back of a highstreet can become a shuttle, mind of its crew,
me, them, and you surrounding that sleeping stranger, a circuit –
shared dream of what this world can be, and believe it, and be lifted.

listening to Cynthia Erivo cover Elvis Presley

and halfway through the third time through
I reheard the you she sings as me. *I can't help*
falling in love with me... 198 seconds of space
to find the same grace; fingers tracing wrinkles
my lips made: tips to cheeks, palms to beard,
my whole body ringing like some fleshy bell.
how starved we are to be held. I knelt below
a window's white veil whispering to a reflection
made of sound: *take my hand. my whole life too.*
this life I fell into like fish food to become a part
of each mind my own mind touches. and later,
holding my dog's matted face in my fist, guiding
a scissor along the delicate skin beneath her eye,
I saw a bus blur by, loaded with souls, gold light
flare in the street; I lay my bare chest against the
kitchen floor and thought: all those years so sure
I'd kill myself, but how inevitable it is to love me.

stitch

once there was a human race
sharing a bowl of warm water.
once there was a den of sheets
draped on kitchen chairs.

once there was a blanket
and a little boy inside it,
on his elbows crawling
through the tunnels of his eyes.

and like felt held on a firework
it was raining light inside him.
and like lavender in steam
it is rising in the man.

nerves knitting new beginnings
to pull soft wool inside them.
now there is an after in you
tomorrow must be gentler.

Notes

The Mark Fisher epigraph is from *all of this is temporary,* a public lecture at Rich Mix, London, recorded in 2016. This book would not be possible without his prophetic spirit and work. The Guy Madden line is quoted from his 2007 'docu-fantasia' *My Winnipeg.*

I.

'sanctuary' and 'puppet' were originally written for inclusion in a group performance with the Hippodrome Young Poets Collective at the 2020 National Youth Poetry Showcase. An excerpt of 'hunger' was displayed at London Bridge for National Poetry Day 2021.

II.

An earlier version of section II was performed as part of *UK Young Artists Takeover 2019.* 'wet-plate process' responds to the work of photography pioneer Eadweard Muybridge and abstracts a zoopraxiscope as its form. 'time spun loosely into a beautiful day' is dedicated to Birmingham poet Leon Priestnall; it features lyrics from the musical *Hair* written by James Rado and Gerome Ragini.

III.

'fresco' was co-commissioned by Overhear and Medicine Bakery Gallery for the 2019 Birmingham Literature Festival; it riffs on a line from Lorca's poem 'Romance Sonámbulo.' 'listening to Cynthia Erivo cover Elvis Presley' refers to a performance of 'Can't Help Falling in Love'; the poem features lyrics to the song written by Hugo Peretti, Luigi Creatore, and George David Weiss. 'stitch' is indebted to a line from James S Holmes' poem 'End of Autumn,' featured in the anthology *Persistent Voices: Poetry by Writers Lost to AIDS.*

Acknowledgements and Thanks

I am grateful to the editors of the following publications in which some of these poems first appeared:

Impossible Archetype: 'has it become any easier to love each other?' *StepAway*: 'night-walking in Exeter'. *A&U: America's AIDS Magazine*: 'song of the first men'. *Magma*: 'underground'. *Eighty-Four: Poems on Male Suicide* (Verve): 'hold me warm blooded thing'.

*

I would like to thank Professor Regenia Gagnier at the University of Exeter who affirmed my initial exploration of poetry's role in staging the 'effective antagonisms' to capitalist realism Fisher lays out for us in his work, and Dr. Felicity Gee for widening my lens on Time, Space, and Identity. I would also like to thank Elizabeth 'Zeddie' Lawal and Mathilde Pethord for opportunity and belief, Uni*Slam for encouraging many young writer-performers, and poetry organisers and audiences across the UK for generous use of the love-filled laboratory; Apples and Snakes and Jerwood Arts for financial support to read, refine, and finish writing; Jonathan Davidson for professional guidance; Chris for importing books before I could afford them; and all the other libraries, brick or flesh: Sean Fitzpatrick for vipassana, anarchism, and LSD; Birmingham Buddhist Centre's warm welcome; Dhamma Dipa's woods to walk in (editing in my head); Sachal Khan for blagging it beside me on stage with a guitar; the attentive minds of Roma Havers, Sean Colletti, Elizabeth Burrell, Nafeesa Hamid, Beth Pitcher, and Josh Leach; Jane Commane, your quiet genius; Lucy for the haircuts; Mum for the shelter; Dad for the clumsy drunken push on the swing toward the dharma; and you, for reading, letting me into your life – I wish us all peace. Lend a copy to someone who needs it.